# THE

## THAT ASTO

# THE APPLE

# THAT ASTONISHED PARIS

---

*poems by Billy Collins*

---

THE UNIVERSITY OF ARKANSAS PRESS

FAYETTEVILLE     1988     LONDON

Copyright © 1988 by Billy Collins
All rights reserved
Manufactured in Canada

04   03   02                    10   9   8

*Designer:* Chiquita Babb
*Typeface:* Linotron 202 Zapf Book Light
*Typesetter:* G & S Typesetters, Inc.

☉   The paper used in this publication meets the
minimum requirements of the American National
Standard for Permanence of Paper for Printed Library
Materials Z39.48-1984.

*Library of Congress Cataloging-in-Publication Data*

Collins, Billy.
    The apple that astonished Paris / Billy Collins.
        p.    cm.
    ISBN 1-55728-023-1 (alk. paper).    ISBN 1-55728-024-X
(pbk. : alk. paper)
    I. Title
PS3553.047478A8    1988
811.'.54—dc19                              87-24191
                                              CIP

# ACKNOWLEDGMENTS

Some of these poems or earlier versions of them have appeared in the following publications: *Crosscurrents, Electrum, Florida Review, The Literary Review, The Midatlantic Review, The Montana Review, Mudfish, The New Yorker, The Pacific Review, Poetry New York, River City Review, Sierra Madre Review, Wooster Review,* and *Wormwood Review.*

"Books" and "Winter Syntax" appeared originally in *Poetry.*

The author is grateful to the New York Foundation for the Arts for a poetry fellowship which helped in the completion of this book.

*For my mother and father*

# CONTENTS

# I

# AWAY

---

# VANISHING POINT

"With an apple I want to astonish Paris."
        —*Paul Cézanne*

You thought it was just a pencil dot
art students made in the middle of the canvas
before they started painting the barn, cows, haystacks,

or just a point where railroad tracks fuse,
a spot engineers stare at from the cabs of trains
as they clack through the heat of prairies
heading out of the dimensional.

But here I am at the vanishing point,
looking back at everything as it zooms toward me,
barns, cows, tracks, haystacks, farmers, the works,
shrinking, then disappearing into this iota
as if pulled by a gravity that is horizontal.

I am a catcher behind the home plate of the world,
a scientist observing a little leak in reality.

I watch the history of architecture narrow down
to nothing, all straight lines rushing away from
themselves like men who have caught on fire.
Every monument since Phidias converges on this speck.
Imagine a period that could swallow all the sentences
in an encyclopedia.

I have reached the heaven of geometry
where every line in every theorem aspires to go.
Even the vanishing points in drawings vanish here.
And if you do not believe me, look at where
the tangents of your garage are aimed.

You have heard of the apple that astonished Paris?
This is the nostril of the ant that inhaled the universe.

# WALKING ACROSS
# THE ATLANTIC

I wait for the holiday crowd to clear the beach
before stepping onto the first wave.

Soon I am walking across the Atlantic
thinking about Spain,
checking for whales, waterspouts.

I feel the water holding up my shifting weight.
Tonight I will sleep on its rocking surface.

But for now I try to imagine what
this must look like to the fish below,
the bottoms of my feet appearing, disappearing.

# THE BLUE

You can have Egypt and Nantucket.
The only place I want to visit is The Blue,
not the Wild Blue Yonder that seduces pilots,
but that zone where the unexpected dwells,
waiting to come out of it in the shape of bolts.

I want to walk its azure perimeter
where the unanticipated is coiled, on the mark,
ready to spring into the predictable homes of earth.

I want to stroll through the pale indigo light
examining all the accidents about to rocket into time,
all the forgotten names about to fly from tongues.

I will scrutinize all the surprises of the future
and watch the brainstorms gathering darkly,
ready to hit the heads of inventors
laboring in their crackpot shacks.

A jaded traveler with an invisible passport,
I am at home in this heaven of the unforeseen
waiting for the next whoosh of sudden departure
when, with no advance warning, no tiny augury,
the unpredictable plummets into our lives
from somewhere that looks like sky.

# SCHOOLSVILLE

Glancing over my shoulder at the past,
I realize the number of students I have taught
is enough to populate a small town.

I can see it nestled in a paper landscape,
chalk dust flurrying down in winter,
nights dark as a blackboard.

The population ages but never graduates.
On hot afternoons they sweat the final in the park
and when it's cold they shiver around stoves
reading disorganized essays out loud.
A bell rings on the hour and everybody zigzags
into the streets with their books.

I forgot all their last names first and their
first names last in alphabetical order.
But the boy who always had his hand up
is an alderman and owns the haberdashery.
The girl who signed her papers in lipstick
leans against the drugstore, smoking,
brushing her hair like a machine.

Their grades are sewn into their clothes
like references to Hawthorne.
The A's stroll along with other A's.
The D's honk whenever they pass another D.

All the creative writing students recline
on the courthouse lawn and play the lute.
Wherever they go, they form a big circle.

Needless to say, I am the mayor.
I live in the white colonial at Maple and Main.
I rarely leave the house. The car deflates
in the driveway. Vines twirl around the porch swing.

Once in a while a student knocks on the door
with a term paper fifteen years late
or a question about Yeats or double-spacing.
And sometimes one will appear in a windowpane
to watch me lecturing the wallpaper,
quizzing the chandelier, reprimanding the air.

# DRIVING WITH ANIMALS

I drive this road that whips through woods at night
always searching ahead for the reflective eyes of deer
who will venture onto the grassy verge to browse.

Winter-snug in the warm interior of the car,
I am speeding in the vague nowhere between places,
an arithmetic problem in space and time
which passes slowly on this long solo haul.
I feed cassettes into the dash, light cigarettes,
check the softly lit panel of instruments
measuring motion, pressure, heat, the arcana of the
    engine,
but there is no red needle to indicate deer.

If I drill my eyes into the night long enough
I will hallucinate shapes in pockets of darkness,
not only deer peering from the fringe of trees,
but other anomalous animals: bison, zebra, even
fish floating in the dreamy pools of fog,

animals released from the mind's deep zoo,
animals we think we see in passing clouds
and in the connected dots of constellations.
Animals parading through the greenery of Eden,
animals on the turning pages of storybooks.
And always deer stepping from the sanctuary of woods,
bolting across the hard ribbon of road in shock,
locked in death-leaps in the sparkle of headlights.

At home as the motor cools in the driveway,
I will feel these rhythms in the quiet of the house.
I will see the heads of deer in the darkened bedroom
and a white flick of tail in the dresser mirror.
I will dream of the sensational touch of a buck's fur
and rock to sleep in the bow and lift of antlers.

# STRANGE LANDS

The photographs of the summer trip are spread
across the table now like little mirrors
reflecting our place in European history.

They are the booty of travel, bordered and colorful,
split seconds that we pass to friends after dinner
one by one to make them believe we really found
some sweet elsewhere, away from here.

There we are, the familiar gazing out of the foreign,
stopped in front of a carved Cistercian door,
or leaning obliquely against a kiosk;
frozen behind a blue and white Della Robbia,
or parked at a café table strewn with phrasebooks,
obscured there in the underexposed shadow of an
    awning.

The waiter in the background, mustache and apron,
is carrying a tray of drinks to others even now
as we flip through the stack another time,
noticing how we tried to be as still as paintings
until the quick rustle of the shutter released us

to walk on again, unfocused, unphotographed,
moving down a street of flowerboxes, motorcycles,
two blurs in the weakening light of evening,
black cameras capped, swaying blindly at our sides.

# TUSCANY

They say wild boar come up from the woods
some nights to drink from the swimming pool

and there are green snakes alive in the fields,
they say, long as a bathrobe cord,
so be careful when you walk down there
with your basket to pick wild flowers.

I even saw one zigzag across the driveway
like a long green charge of electricity,
but I think more about the hard-bristled boar
drinking from the jasmined pool where we swim
our vacation away in the long afternoons.

And when it is too hot to sleep I picture one,
its brutish shape bent over the white edge,
the inflatable toys bobbing at the deep end,
as it laps the dark water and lifts its head,
the tusks dripping in moonlight.

It is the same *cinghiale* we see in the village,
its name printed on the restaurant menu,
its thighs pierced by the butcher's hooks,
its head, nailed to a board in the bar,
glaring from the wall above the crooked table
where the local hunters are playing cards.

# TOURIST: DROMAHAIR, CO. SLIGO

After dinner you stroll from the hotel
through this village that could be an allegory
with its single barbershop, single laundry,
its one-of-each simplicity, free of duplication.
Everything here begins with a capital letter.

The evening hangs in the air like lace
which stirs with river breeze as you cross the bridge,
walking the length of the one street
until it broadens at each end into outbound roads
which channel cars through the darkness
and empty them into the light of other towns.

You pass the Garage, Butchershop, Milliner's,
a place for every nameable need, taste, whimsy,
then the Library stacked with complication
and the Church housing its single idea.

The inhabitants could pose for a group photograph
that could be called Humanity, babies included,
you think as you head for the one pub.

You, of course, would be the photographer—
head and shoulders shrouded by the black cloth,
palm raised to tell them to hold still and smile—
not in the picture, but still a part of all
that your lens and mirrors turn upside down.

# FLYING TO A FUNERAL

A realm of the visible world rolls below
changing colors like a map on a table top
as we inch north at hundreds of miles an hour.
Through the oval membrane of the window
I see only places from which he is absent:
suburban diagrams where he is not plunging
into the blue dot of a swimming pool;
checkerboard farms where he is not leading
a horse into the darkness of a barn
or even driving along, honking at cows;
and now, as the chord of jet engines lowers,
Montreal's park-green patterns, unstrolled
by him and river bridges no longer crossed.
I imagine rinks of ice down there,
unimpressed by the cut of his skates
and taverns minus the tune of his voice.
He is nowhere in these or any other places.

The night I heard the insulting facts
(18 years old, playing hockey, heart attack)
I remember leaning over in a darkening garden
to whiff, as if in his behalf, white lilac
blossoms loaded with cool evening rain,
then biting down on one hard, reeling with its taste,
alive there under the low, harboring clouds.

## ETYMOLOGY

They call Basque an orphan language.
Linguists do not know
what other languages gave it birth.

From the high window of the orphanage
it watches English walking alone to the cemetery
to visit the graves of its parents,
Latin and Anglo-Saxon.

# HUNGER

The fox you lug over your shoulder
in a dark sack
has cut a hole with a knife
and escaped.

The sudden lightness makes you think
you are stronger
as you walk back to your small cottage
through a forest that covers the world.

# HART CRANE

This time when I think of his leap
from the railing of a ship
which sailed on, a scale model of the world,

I weigh only the moments when he was caught
first in the wake,
lifted and dropped in its artificial rhythm,

then must have felt the timing change
as the sea's own beat resumed
and made him part of the cadence of its waves,
dark turquoise with rolling white tops.

# WINTER SYNTAX

A sentence starts out like a lone traveler
heading into a blizzard at midnight,
tilting into the wind, one arm shielding his face,
the tails of his thin coat flapping behind him.

There are easier ways of making sense,
the connoisseurship of gesture, for example.
You hold a girl's face in your hands like a vase.
You lift a gun from the glove compartment
and toss it out the window into the desert heat.
These cool moments are blazing with silence.

The full moon makes sense. When a cloud crosses it
it becomes as eloquent as a bicycle leaning
outside a drugstore or a dog who sleeps all afternoon
in a corner of the couch.

Bare branches in winter are a form of writing.
The unclothed body is autobiography.
Every lake is a vowel, every island a noun.

But the traveler persists in his misery,
struggling all night through the deepening snow,
leaving a faint alphabet of bootprints
on the white hills and the white floors of valleys,
a message for field mice and passing crows.

At dawn he will spot the vine of smoke
rising from your chimney, and when he stands
before you shivering, draped in sparkling frost,
a smile will appear in the beard of icicles,
and the man will express a complete thought.

# PLIGHT OF THE TROUBADOUR

For a good hour I have been singing lays
in langue d'oc to a woman who knows
only langue d'oil, an odd Picard dialect
at that.

The European love lyric is flourishing
with every tremor of my voice,
yet a friend has had to tap my shoulder
to tell me she has not caught a word.

My sentiments are tangled like kites
in the branches of her incomprehension,
and soon I will be lost in an anthology
and poets will no longer wear hats like mine.

Provence will be nothing more
than a pink hue on a map or an answer on a test.
And still the woman smiles over at me
feigning this look of sisterly understanding.

# THE FRANKENSTEIN POET

Pursued by the mob of townspeople
and the shaky glow of their torches,
he finds refuge crouching under a mossy bridge.

He takes a notepad from his huge jacket
and feels inspiration arriving
like a forking of electricity.

He fingers one of the wooden pegs
the doctor tapped into his temples,
little handlebars of the imagination now,

and his pencil moves in the darkness
to a jostling of vocabulary.

He is starting to write an elegy
for all the people whose bodies
are now parts of his body.
It opens with the eyes.

# LOST

———

Now that all the road signs have disappeared
people are pulling their cars onto shoulders
and gathering at erased intersections
to wonder in nervous groups which way to go
or should we just wait here for the authorities?

Those with thinking caps put them on their heads.
A man waves a map but it is only a painting of a map.
A child produces a compass but the needle
points only to a distant toy store.
Now they know how the lost continent must have felt,
only on a smaller scale.

The unstable pound their steering wheels.
The rash drive off in any direction,
tail lights fading like the eyes of dying beasts.

That must be west, someone cries, pointing down
at his summer shoes, so east must be up there
where clouds are taking on the shape of tanks.
The rain is cruel, washing away the roads.

This goes on for such a long time
that the people who had been outward bound
start feeling sorry for the ones who were headed home.

Nobody knows where the road signs are hidden,
but by now they must be covered by long grass
as are the small towns whose names they used
to announce with such civility.

# THE PAST

There is no doubt we all had one,
waist-deep as we are in the evidence of diaries,
home movies and strange names in old address books,
not to mention Architecture and Geology,
stone clocks that measure the deeper past.

And we have anecdotes, warped beyond recognition,
and a scar on the chin from a fall,
but nothing to compare with those few vivid moments
which are vivid for no reason at all—
a face at a children's party, or just a blue truck,
moments that have no role in any story,
worthless to a biographer, but mysterious
and rivaling the colors of the present.

Remembering them is like reading a poem
that begins by carrying us, zombie-like,
down basement stairs as if to leave us in the dark
feeling the air for a light cord,

but then a little metaphor begins to grow
with such detail that it becomes a place,
a lake, for instance, cold and pine-bordered,
which we could dive into and feel nothing,
or a sunny white room where we could live
without ever having to be alive.

# FUR

The night is full of the bulldog policemen
who try to enforce order in cartoons,
the heavy-set ones with droopy ears
and three-fingered hands.

They wear long blue coats with gold buttons.
Small, rounded hats with gold stars
sit on their oafish heads.
They run in the dark waving nightsticks.

I am the cat they use for a siren.
They strap him to their squad-car fenders.
They make him howl by cranking his tail.

# FLAMES

Smokey the Bear heads
into the autumn woods
with a red can of gasoline
and a box of wooden matches.

His ranger's hat is cocked
at a disturbing angle.

His brown fur gleams
under the high sun
as his paws, the size
of catcher's mitts,
crackle into the distance.

He is sick of dispensing
warnings to the careless,
the half-wit camper,
the dumbbell hiker.

He is going to show them
how a professional does it.

# II

# HOME

---

# BOOKS

From the heart of this dark, evacuated campus
I can hear the library humming in the night,
a choir of authors murmuring inside their books
along the unlit, alphabetical shelves,
Giovani Pontano next to Pope, Dumas next to his son,
each one stitched into his own private coat,
together forming a low, gigantic chord of language.

I picture a figure in the act of reading,
shoes on a desk, head tilted into the wind of a book,
a man in two worlds, holding the rope of his tie
as the suicide of lovers saturates a page,
or lighting a cigarette in the middle of a theorem.
He moves from paragraph to paragraph
as if touring a house of endless, panelled rooms.

I hear the voice of my mother reading to me
from a chair facing the bed, books about horses and dogs,
and inside her voice lie other distant sounds,
the horrors of a stable ablaze in the night,
a bark that is moving toward the brink of speech.

I watch myself building bookshelves in college,
walls within walls, as rain soaks New England,
or standing in a bookstore in a trench coat.

I see all of us reading ourselves away from ourselves,
straining in circles of light to find more light
until the line of words becomes a trail of crumbs
that we follow across a page of fresh snow;

when evening is shadowing the forest
and small birds flutter down to consume the crumbs,
we have to listen hard to hear the voices
of the boy and his sister receding into the woods.

# ON CLOSING *ANNA KARENINA*

I must have started reading this monster
a decade before Tolstoy was born
but the vodka and the suicide are behind me now,
all the winter farms, ice-skating and horsemanship.

It consumed so many evenings and afternoons,
I thought a Russian official would appear
to slip a medal over my lowered head
when I reached the last page.

But I found there only the last word,
a useless looking thing, stalled there,
ending its sentence and the whole book at once.

With no more plot to nudge along and nothing
to unfold, it is the only word with no future.

It stares into space and chants its own name
as a traveler whose road has just vanished
might stare into the dark, vacant fields ahead,
knowing he cannot go forward, cannot go back.

# INDOORS

I lose perspective in national museums
wandering through the nest of rooms.
I forget that history is a long scroll
floating over a smoky battlefield.
When I bend over a glass case to inspect
the detail on an engraved shield,
I stop at a curlicue as if it were everything.
Then in the rare books room I am mesmerized
by little illustrations in the margins
of dictionaries, ink pictures of a lizard, a kayak.
Lost down a corridor of suits of armor,
I cannot find the daylight of an exit
or even an airy room of outdoor paintings,
no blue sky and white clouds in a gold frame.
Maybe it is time to return to the beginning
of knowledge, to relearn everything quietly,
to open an alphabet book and say to myself,
lips moving silently, A is for Apple.

# DEATH

In the old days news of it traveled by foot.
An aproned woman would wave to her husband
as he receded down the lane, hauling
the stone of the message.

Or someone would bring it out by horse,
a boy galloping, an old man trotting along.
A girl would part a curtain wondering
what anyone would be doing here at this hour,
as he dismounted, hitched the beast to a post,
then lifted the brass knocker, cold as the night.

But today we have the telephone.
You can hear one from where you are right now,
its hammer almost touching the little bell,
ready to summon you, ready to fall from your hand.

# REMEMBERING DREAMS

No one seems to be a champ at this.
We lift from the pillow a head flickering
with the light from an unlikely scene:
we are driving backwards down a highway in space
or searching a house with cockeyed walls for a door,
or stairs, and running into the face of a dead uncle.

But the rest of the story vanishes
as if someone had ripped an ancient epic from our
    hands
leaving us with a fragment, a few hexameters
whose rhythm is drowned out by the beat of daylight.

Just as well we salvage only these scraps,
otherwise we would sit up in bed all day
replaying these strange movies about ourselves,
dumbstruck in pajamas at the escapades that go on
while we toss, snore and kick off blankets.

We would be like enraptured explorers peering
out of a diving bell in the Arctic
beholding the whole measureless iceberg.

# EARTHLING

You have probably come across
those scales in planetariums
that tell you how much you
would weigh on other planets.

You have noticed the fat ones
lingering on the Mars scale
and the emaciated slowing up
the line for Neptune.

As a creature of average weight,
I fail to see the attraction.

Imagine squatting in the wasteland
of Pluto, all five tons of you,
or wandering around Mercury
wondering what to do next with your ounce.

How much better to step onto
the simple bathroom scale,
a happy earthling feeling
the familiar ropes of gravity,

157 pounds standing soaking wet
a respectful distance from the sun.

# CHILD DEVELOPMENT

As sure as prehistoric fish grew legs
and sauntered off the beaches into forests
working up some irregular verbs for their
first conversation, so three-year-old children
enter the phase of name-calling.

Every day a new one arrives and is added
to the repertoire. You Dumb Goopyhead,
You Big Sewerface, You Poop-on-the-Floor
(a kind of Navaho ring to that one)
they yell from knee level, their little mugs
flushed with challenge.
Nothing Samuel Johnson would bother tossing out
in a pub, but then the toddlers are not trying
to devastate some fatuous Enlightenment hack.

They are just tormenting their fellow squirts
or going after the attention of the giants
way up there with their cocktails and bad breath
talking baritone nonsense to other giants,
waiting to call them names after thanking
them for the lovely party and hearing the door close.

The mature save their hothead invective
for things: an errant hammer, tire chains,
or receding trains missed by seconds,
though they know in their adult hearts,
even as they threaten to banish Timmy to bed
for his appalling behavior,
that their bosses are Big Fatty Stupids,
their wives are Dopey Dopeheads
and that they themselves are Mr. Sillypants.

# PUTTING DOWN THE CAT

The assistant holds her on the table,
the fur hanging limp from her tiny skeleton,
and the veterinarian raises the needle of fluid
which will put the line through her ninth life.

"Painless," he reassures me, "like counting
backwards from a hundred," but I want to tell him
that our poor cat cannot count at all,
much less to a hundred, much less backwards.

# THE LESSON

In the morning when I found History
snoring heavily on the couch,
I took down his overcoat from the rack
and placed its weight over my shoulder blades.

It would protect me on the cold walk
into the village for milk and the paper
and I figured he would not mind,
not after our long conversation the night before.

How unexpected his blustering anger
when I returned covered with icicles,
the way he rummaged through the huge pockets
making sure no major battle or English queen
had fallen out and become lost in the deep snow.

# LOWELL, MASS.

Kerouac was born in the same town
as my father, but my father never
had time to write *On the Road*

let alone drive around the country
in circles.

He wrote notes for the kitchen table
and a novel of checks
and a few speeches to lullaby
businessmen after a fat lunch

and some of his writing is within
me for I house catalogues of jokes
and handbooks of advice
on horses, snow tires, women,

along with some short stories
about the deadbeats at the office,
but he was quicker to pick up
a telephone than a pen.

Like Jack, he took a drink but
beatific to him meant the Virgin Mary.

He called jazz jungle music
and he would have told Neal Cassady
to let him off at the next light.

# PROGRAMS

Even the earth I am balancing on feels thin,
like a page of colors in an enormous atlas,
and the horizon is the edge of a book
someone is reading in another city.

The world is hiding in back of itself,
the walls and leaves, cars and furniture
all inches out of reach although my arms
are outheld like a sleepwalker's.

And the noises that remind me I am breathing
here—ambulance siren, thunder, creaking door—
sound like sound effects on an old radio mystery
listened to in the shadowy bedrooms of childhood.

When I believed in everything, I could not see
the actors semicircled around a studio microphone
flipping the pages of scripts in unison.
I only heard the voices, resonant, electric, adult,
accusing each other of murder.

# THE MORNING AFTER MY DEATH

On the morning that follows my death, the sun
will no doubt rise through the slats of these pines
and paint its usual light on the east end of the house,
on the white garden gate and on my useless car,
unless, of course, it happens to be raining,

in which case these windows will be maps of water,
the roof will be the weather's melancholic drum
and low gray clouds will sweep over this neighborhood.

What's more, the men along this street will leave
for the train station holding black umbrellas
like thin rare mushrooms shining with rain.

I can see one of them clearly now, walking
along with a newspaper tucked under his arm.
He has cut himself shaving and a bit of tissue
with a circle of blood is stuck to his cheek,

and as he walks, blood is pulsing
along his arteries and their tributaries, the veins,
and up the tiniest of capillaries, each one
like a remote jungle river unexplored by anyone
except the hermit who lives in a hut on its quiet bank.

# PERSONAL HISTORY

"I would
love you ten years before the flood"
—*Andrew Marvell*

A long time ago when cataclysms were common
as sneezes and land masses slid
around the globe looking for places
to settle down and become continents,
someone introduced us at a party.

Later on, as the Renaissance flowered,
I fell in love with you, egged on by the sonnet
and the idea of your individuality.

We married during the Industrial Revolution,
coughing on a brown lawn above a city
humming with flywheels and drive belts.
The ceremony went like clockwork.

When war rattled the world, we shut the blinds
and huddled under a table while sirens harmonized.
Everything but our affection was rationed.

Now we find ourselves in the post-modern age,
using one of its many Saturday nights
to drive to the movies in a Volkswagen.

"It doesn't seem we've been together that long,"
you say, looking at my profile,
contracting the past into the rearview mirror,
beaming the future into the tunneling of our headlights.

# BAR TIME

In keeping with universal saloon practice,
the clock here is set fifteen minutes ahead
of all the clocks in the outside world.

This makes us a rather advanced group,
doing our drinking in the unknown future,
immune from the cares of the present,
safely harbored a quarter of an hour
beyond the woes of the contemporary scene.

No wonder such thoughtless pleasure derives
from tending the small fire of a cigarette,
from observing this glass of whiskey and ice,
the cold rust I am sipping,

or from having an eye on the street outside
when Ordinary Time slouches past in a topcoat,
rain running off the brim of his hat,
the late edition like a flag in his pocket.

# INSOMNIA

After counting all the sheep in the world
I enumerate the wildebeests, snails,
camels, skylarks, etc.,

then I add up all the zoos and aquariums,
country by country.

By early light I am asleep
in a nightmare about drowning in the Flood,
yelling across the rising water
at preoccupied Noah as his wondrous
ark sails by and begins to grow smaller.

Now a silhouette on the horizon,
the only boat on earth is disappearing.

As I rise and fall on the rocking waves,
I concentrate on the giraffe couple,
their necks craning over the roof,
to keep my life from flashing before me.

After all the animals wink out of sight
I float on my back, eyes closed.
I picture all the fish in creation
leaping a fence in a field of water,
one colorful species after another.

# ANOTHER REASON WHY
# I DON'T KEEP A GUN IN THE HOUSE

The neighbors' dog will not stop barking.
He is barking the same high, rhythmic bark
that he barks every time they leave the house.
They must switch him on on their way out.

The neighbors' dog will not stop barking.
I close all the windows in the house
and put on a Beethoven symphony full blast
but I can still hear him muffled under the music,
barking, barking, barking,

and now I can see him sitting in the orchestra,
his head raised confidently as if Beethoven
had included a part for barking dog.

When the record finally ends he is still barking,
sitting there in the oboe section barking,
his eyes fixed on the conductor who is
entreating him with his baton

while the other musicians listen in respectful
silence to the famous barking dog solo,
that endless coda that first established
Beethoven as an innovative genius.

# CANCER

When you need to say the word,
it cowers in back of your vocabulary
behind some outdated slang.

And if you try forcing it into the mouth
it lodges in the throat like a fishbone.

My father cannot say it yet.
The old man cannot even hear it.
He pretends I am saying "campfire."

# EMBRACE

You know the parlor trick.
Wrap your arms around your own body
and from the back it looks like
someone is embracing you,
her hands grasping your shirt,
her fingernails teasing your neck.

From the front it is another story.
You never looked so alone,
your crossed elbows and screwy grin.
You could be waiting for a tailor
to fit you for a straitjacket,
one that would hold you really tight.

# THE RIVAL POET

The column of your book titles,
always introducing your latest one,
looms over me like Roman architecture.

It is longer than the name
of an Italian countess, longer
than this poem will probably be.

Etched on the head of a pin,
my own production would leave room for
The Lord's Prayer and many dancing angels.
No matter.

In my revenge daydream I am the one
poised on the marble staircase
high above the crowded ballroom.
A retainer in livery announces me
and the Contessa Maria Teresa Isabella
Veronica Multalire Eleganza de Bella Ferrari.

You are the one below
fidgeting in your rented tux
with some local Cindy hanging all over you.

# MY NUMBER

Is Death miles away from this house,
reaching for a widow in Cincinnati
or breathing down the neck of a lost hiker
in British Columbia?

Is he too busy making arrangements,
tampering with air brakes,
scattering cancer cells like seeds,
loosening the wooden beams of roller coasters

to bother with my hidden cottage
that visitors find so hard to find?

Or is he stepping from a black car
parked at the dark end of the lane,
shaking open the familiar cloak,
its hood raised like the head of a crow,
and removing the scythe from the trunk?

Did you have any trouble with the directions?
I will ask, as I start talking my way out of this.

# POEM

Some poems name their subjects.
The titles are *On* this or *On* that,
or they hang like small marquees
indicating what is playing inside:
"Celibacy," "Ostriches at Dusk."

Other poems fall into it as they go along.
You trip over a word while carrying
a tray of vocabulary out to the pool
only to discover that broken glass
is a good topic.

Still others have no subject
other than themselves to gnaw on.
The fly lands on the swatter.
The movie runs backwards
and catches fire in the projector.
This species apes us well
by talking only about itself.

Such is often the case with poems
afflicted by the same plain title
as this one:
a sign by the road announcing a bump.

# HOPELESS BUT NOT SERIOUS

These days every morning begins like a joke
you think you have heard before,
but there is no one telling it whom you can stop.

One day it's about a cow who walks into a bar,
then about a man with a big nose on his honeymoon,
then about a kangaroo who walks into a bar.
Each one takes up an entire day.

The sun looks like a prank Nathanael West
is pulling on the world; on the drive to work
cars are swinging comically from lane to lane.
The houses and lawns belong in cartoons.

The hours collapse into one another's arms.
The stories arc over noon and descend
like slow ferris wheels into the haze of evening.
You wish you could stop listening and get serious.

Trouble is you cannot remember the punch line
which never arrives until very late at night,
just as you are reaching over for the bedside lamp,
just before you begin laughing in the dark.

# ADVICE TO WRITERS

Even if it keeps you up all night,
wash down the walls and scrub the floor
of your study before composing a syllable.

Clean the place as if the Pope were on his way.
Spotlessness is the niece of inspiration.

The more you clean, the more brilliant
your writing will be, so do not hesitate to take
to the open fields to scour the undersides
of rocks or swab in the dark forest
upper branches, nests full of eggs.

When you find your way back home
and stow the sponges and brushes under the sink,
you will behold in the light of dawn
the immaculate altar of your desk,
a clean surface in the middle of a clean world.

From a small vase, sparkling blue, lift
a yellow pencil, the sharpest of the bouquet,
and cover pages with tiny sentences
like long rows of devoted ants
that followed you in from the woods.

# INTRODUCTION TO POETRY

I ask them to take a poem
and hold it up to the light
like a color slide

or press an ear against its hive.

I say drop a mouse into a poem
and watch him probe his way out,

or walk inside the poem's room
and feel the walls for a light switch.

I want them to waterski
across the surface of a poem
waving at the author's name on the shore.

But all they want to do
is tie the poem to a chair with rope
and torture a confession out of it.

They begin beating it with a hose
to find out what it really means.

# DESIRE

It would be easier to compile an encyclopedia
for you than to write these longhand letters
whose ink blackens the night. I write
until dawn saying I think the world of you

but they are always too short
like those two-page schoolboy essays
with *The History of Mankind*
underlined on the front in crayon.

My encyclopedia will ignore the research
of others and rely on personal experience.

I will walk out the front door now
with my winter hat and coat,
with my spectacles and my knotty cane.
I will describe in a clear, nimble style
everything in the world beginning with A.

# THE BROOKLYN MUSEUM OF ART

I will now step over the soft velvet rope
and walk directly into this massive Hudson River
painting and pick my way along the Palisades
with this stick I snapped off a dead tree.

I will skirt the smoky, nestled towns
and seek the path that leads always outward
until I become lost, without a hope
of ever finding the way back to the museum.

I will stand on the bluffs in nineteenth-century clothes,
a dwarf among rock, hills and flowing water,
and I will fish from the banks in a straw hat
which will feel like a brush stroke on my head.

And I will hide in the green covers of forests
so no appreciator of Frederick Edwin Church,
leaning over the soft velvet rope,
will spot my tiny figure moving in the stillness
and cry out, pointing for the others to see,

and be thought mad and led away to a cell
where there is no vaulting landscape to explore,
none of this bird song that halts me in my tracks,
and no wide curving of this river that draws
my steps toward the misty vanishing point.